The Best Small Book of . . .

Bars in
NEW
YORK

By HOWARD COOPER

First published in Great Britain in 2007 by
© Summer of 77 Productions
e-mail: summerof77@supanet.com

Text © Howard Cooper
Photographs © Howard Cooper
Design and layout © Mike Nicholson

ISBN 978-0-9554334-0-5

A catalogue record for this book is
available from the British Library.

Printed and bound by
Creative Image, Newcastle

Contents

NEW YORK is the greatest city on the planet. Anyone who tries to tell you any different is wrong. Everything you've ever seen, heard or read about it is true.

We all heart NY. We've visited it a thousand times through TV shows and the movies, and yet nothing can ever prepare you for the sheer heart-pounding thrill of the place. And it never wears off, no matter how many times you visit.

But if you really want to take a bite out of the Big Apple, you'll want to know where to wash it down.

There are hundreds of places to get a drink and there's something for

everyone. And we've tried to keep everyone happy.

You might want history or romance; a watering hole near a tourist attraction; live football or somewhere with a kick-ass view.

Chances are this guide will leave you with a hang over. What it won't do is leave you queuing outside a place on a freezing January night, praying the guy with the clipboard sees how fabulous you are and unhooks the velvet rope.

Several of NYC's hottest nightspots didn't make it because of their over-zealous entrance policies. **See, we can be just as picky about who we let in.**

YOU MUST TIP. It's that simple. You might not tip the student at the Dog and Duck but if you don't pony up the dough in America you'll never get served in that bar again.

Think of it as the First Rule of Fight Club. And the Second Rule of Fight Club is - you must tip! The going rate is $1 a drink and 15 per cent for meals.

Now if you want to start a tab in a bar they'll want your credit card, even if you don't plan to pay with plastic. If you do use your flexible friend to settle up don't add your tip to the total; give the bartender cash. They'll appreciate it as it saves them messing about with tills - and the Tax Man.

The majority of bartenders in the USA are professionals:

Some sound advice

it's what they do for a living, not what they do to get some extra cash for Christmas. They work like dogs, the money's pants and the hours are long. That's why tips are so important.

A good bartender will remember your order, spot you through a three-deep-bar, check on you when your glass is getting low - and give you freebies. If you've tipped on your first three drinks you can pretty much expect your fourth will be gratis.

The legal drinking age in America is 21 and it's a good idea to carry your passport as proof of age, even if you're blatantly older.

At some point you will be asked for ID. Yes it seems ridiculous and even flattering but as you'll be told when you ask if they're joking: "It ain't for your benefit."

Smoking in New York's bars and restaurants has been banned since March 2003. With the exception of a handful of establishments in the city, if you want to spark up you'll have to go outside. But fear not as we know where some Super King-friendly spots are.

The majority of bars in New York stay open until 4am but if you plan to wake up with a hangover in the City That Never Sleeps remember you're a visitor and all the cops have guns - and Tasers.

Enjoy your drink responsibly and never drink and drive.

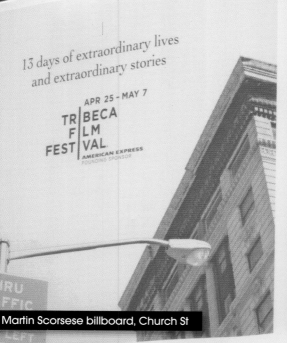

Martin Scorsese billboard, Church St

Bubble Lounge

Take me to: 228 W. Broadway (between Franklin & North Moore Sts)

FORMULA ONE would be a much more interesting sport if instead of just shaking their champers, popping the cork and letting rip, they lopped the top off with a sabre.

The Bubble Lounge is the first New York member of the prestigious "confrerie du sabre d'or", a brotherhood dating back to Napoleon's time. Boney's mounted troops would regularly celebrate their return from combat by decapitating a few bottles of bubbly to arouse the ladies. This impressive opening ceremony is available right here and the Lounge's blade hangs behind the bar, awaiting its call to arms.

There are two entrances to the L-shaped Bubble Lounge, with the North Moore door really the tradesmans and the bar sitting in the elbow of the L. The tiled floor is covered with plump sofas and chairs, and mirrors, paintings and bubbly ads adorn the brick walls.

As you'd expect, there's a huge choice of champagnes and sparkling wines. Light-bodied, full-bodied, rose and demi-sec; Laurent-Perrier, Taittinger, Bollinger, Veuve Clicquot, Krug, Moet & Chandon; even Francis Coppola Sofia Blanc de Blancs 2003.

Downstairs sits The Krug Room, a cool and classy cellar with a separate bar.

Nibbles include oysters, caviar, or a cheese platter. And don't forget to tip at least 15 per cent. Remember, there's a sword behind the bar.

Brandy Library

Take me to: 25 North Moore St (at Varick St)

YOU know how they like you to keep the noise down in libraries, well this shrine to the amber nectars is no different as Hollywood tough guy Harvey Keitel has been down to complain about the noise.

The star of Oscar-winner The Piano popped in at 2am to have polite words as a tipsy reveller was keeping his young family awake with a drunken rendition of "Chopsticks" on the Library's upright.

Pulp Fiction's Mr Wolf lives in a loft above Brandy Library, which is housed in the famous 100-year-old Atalanta Building. The place was just an empty shell before owner Flavien Desoblin founded this unique outlet for his passion for brown liquors in October 2004.

The bottles are housed on back-lit shelves that come complete with ladders on brass rails. Brown velour banquettes are lined up opposite and low, comfy leather chairs are positioned around glass-topped tables. The lighting and decor are as warm as the booze and the jazz soundtrack never intrudes.

There are over 400 bottles of cognac and armagnac, 250 single malts, 60-odd bourbons and 50 rums. Drinks are served in stemless Riedel "O" glasses, except for cocktails and champers, which are poured in classic saucers.

The whole point of a library is to educate and the staff - headed by spirit sommelier Ethan R. Kelley - can guide you through your choices. C'est bon.

Ulysses'

Take me to: 95 Pearl St/58 Stone St (at Hanover Sq)

BROUGHT to you by the people behind Swift and Puck Fair, Ulysses' is nearly as big as James Joyce's novel - but a lot more fun. A short walk from Wall Street, it really is the only party in this part of town, which is fine as the crowd in here like a knees-up.

This cavernous boozer covers the block between Stone and Pearl Streets. Whichever doorway you pick you'll find yourself in a loud, dark, bustling "rockbound house of joy", complete with a DJ. Visit on a Friday after the Market closes and you might hear Depeche Mode.

Ulysses' is all exposed brick and wood, and is split into two rooms. The first houses a huge 360-degree bar, while the second - called the Swift Carvery - is more geared to groups with its high tables and stools.

The bar is armed with draught Guinness and Boddies, plus 12 other beers on tap and more spirits than A Christmas Carol. There's stools aplenty and booths for you and your "messmates" to unwind in - or take stock, if you'll pardon the pun. No prizes for guessing it's busy after work and if things are too cosy for you inside, you can mount a hostile takeover of a bench on Stone St.

Pictures of Joyce down the ages line the walls and it doesn't matter whether he was a sailor-suited toddler or moustachioed author, he always looked stressed.

Smile, you miserable bugger! There's a great bar named in your honour.

Corner of Broadway & W. Houston St

SoHo

2

Broome Street Bar

Take me to: 363 W. Broadway (corner of Broome St)

NOT so far from the madding crowds of stick-thin x-rays, luvvies and fashionistas who inhabit the designer-shop and art-gallery enclave of SoHo, is a little bar offering cold beer, hot food and a warm welcome.

Broome Street is run by octogenarian Kenn Reisdorff, a Seattle-born former actor who trained in London before moving to NYC in 1954.

The classic SoHo structure dates back to 1825 and was a sleaze joint and then an Italian restaurant until Kenn and brother Bob took over in 1972. The restaurant went bust after the owner shot and killed a punter for sleeping with his girlfriend, only to be shot dead himself by his victim's brother.

Kenn wanted a place where his artist pals could hang out and describes it as a "very unpretentious US bar". Black walls, a bare plank floor, arse-worn stools and tables with red-and-white check table cloths sit in full view of the shoppers, who totter past the large windows facing West Broadway.

Broome Street's menu and beer selections are written on blackboards, with Bud, Guinness, Brooklyn Lager and Dogfish Head Ale in pints; Warsteiner, London Pride and Hoegaarden in bottles.

The impressive stained glass window is displayed behind the bar. Kenn bought it years ago, originally for his home. The Blue Boy, as he's known, is something of a mystery but has become the bar's logo.

Circa Tabac

Take me to: 32 Watts St (between W. Broadway & 6th Ave)

ON MARCH 30, 2003, Mayor Michael Bloomberg's Smoker-Free City Act came into force. Anyone caught sparking up in a bar or restaurant could be arrested, fined $100 and also banged up for 30 days.

But rejoice and take in deep lungfuls of really harmful smoke, because Circa Tabac is NYC's **ONLY** cigarette lounge. Instead of being forced to stand outside in the cold, huddled around a Woodbine for warmth, you can happily fur up your arteries under the shade of a plastic palm in this Art Deco-inspired lounge.

The majority of the space is devoted to seating, be it banquettes, chairs at the bar and windows, or small tables for four. And there's surprisingly few burn holes in the seats.

Circa Tabac has a menu of 150 different types of cigarettes. Ditch the Silk Cut and light up a Jezebel, an Al Capone, or a Black Death. There's also a good food menu, which includes filet mignon en croissant.

Booze includes the Circa Tabac cocktail, a cheeky mix of cognac, Grand Marnier, honey and lemon juice; or the Apricot Bastard, which is made from apricot brandy and bubbly.

A word of warning: the draughts don't come in pints. The stemmed glasses are elegant, but are just over an half - for the price of a pint everywhere else. But while everywhere else has full measures of Wife Beater, Circa Tabac has ashtrays.

Ear Inn

Take me to: 326 Spring St (between Greenwich & Washington Sts)

THIS cosy little smugglers' den is a genuine piece of American history and was built in 1817 for an African-American called James Brown. Not the Godfather of Soul, but the JB who was an aide to George Washington during the Revolution and is reportedly pictured in the famous painting of the future President crossing the Delaware.

The James Brown House became a bar in the mid-19th Century. The upstairs was also a brothel at one point, frequented by sailors who found themselves in port when there was a storm.

To many it's still the Green Door, and only became the Ear Inn in 1977 when the B on the neon BAR sign outside was altered with paint in honour of the Ear Magazine, a music mag published upstairs.

Venture in of an afternoon - Saturdays there are poetry readings - and you'll encounter weathered regulars supping a hair o' the dog, salty sea dogs spinning yarns - and plenty of British accents.

Mobiles are banned but there's a payphone by the door, by the shelf with the huge dictionary that's used for settling arguments.

Davy Jones doesn't have a locker here but you're welcome to dump your coats and bags on the bench by the phone.

At the bar you'll find Boddies, Stella, Harp and Bass on tap, plus spirits. There's even one called Mickey that haunts the place; the ghost of a long-dead sailor waiting for his ship to come in.

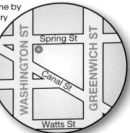

Puck Fair

Take me to: 298 Lafayette St (between Houston & Prince Sts)

WHEN the fair's in town you always want to go, right? This aircraft hangar of a pub sits on the top edge of SoHo and is a handy spot to dump the shopping bags and sink a pint during a spot of retail therapy.

The writing on the wall proclaims: "Kings may come and kings may go...but King Puck goes on forever". It all seems a bit Tolkieny for a billie goat, but that's what this Irish bar is named after.

This big-for-her-age little sister of Ulysses' and Swift spans the entire block between Crosby and Lafayette, with the actual bar just a few feet short at both ends.

All the walls behind the bar are decorated with Gaelic lyrics and "The Legend of Puck Fair", while opposite sit wooden booths. At the bottom end is a mezzanine that seats about 20, plus a DJ and his vinyl. All this beneath the vertigo-inducing 30ft-high ceiling. Downstairs is the Gate Bar, which is open from 6pm-4am.

Luckily for some there's 13 draught beers to whet your whistle, including Boddies, IPA, Stella and Guinness; while the fridges house 46 different bottled beers.

Puck Fair's bartenders are friendly in that pleased-you-popped-in Irish way, the place is always lively, there's occasional live music and also live football on the tele every now and then.

Now isn't all that better than a goldfish in a bag and a spin on the dodgems?

9/11 memorial, 7th Ave Sth & Greenwich Ave

West Village &
Meatpacking District

Chumley's

Take me to: 86 Bedford St (between Barrow and Grove Sts)

AS MUCH a Waterstone's as a watering hole, Chumley's used to serve the likes of John Steinbeck, Jack Kerouac, Bob Dylan and Millers Henry and Arthur. The walls are plastered with pictures of its famous literary libators and copies of their books' covers.

Blink and you'll miss this former speakeasy as the only thing that lets you know it's there is an unmarked doorway with a heavy wooden door. But once you toddle up the steps and step through the curtain down into its granite-walled interior, you'll come over all secretive and never breath a word about it.

The first section is a restaurant of wooden booths, with the bar in the second room. Old-fashioned beer taps poke out from a copper wall and offer such treats as Bud Light, Chumley's Eagle Pilsner, Chumley's Bulldog Bitter and Chumley's Labrador Lager.

Leland Stanford Chumley opened the bar in 1928. Rumoured to be a serial swordsman, Lee allegedly hopped in and out of many beds but kept one free for the Chief of Police, who rented the upstairs at Chumley's during Prohibition.

Before a raid the Chief would phone the bar and simply say "86", and the revellers would scarper through a fake bookcase before the rozzers arrived.

To this day there are "86" lists in kitchens, used by the chef to write down everything they're out of.

The Cubbyhole

Take me to: 281 W. 12th St (at 4th St)

REMEMBER that snug little place you used to curl up in as a kid? Well this cosy lesbian bar will have you reaching for your blankie. And you might even get to suck someone else's thumb if your lucky.

Gay bars are usually men only, fag hags and the confused, but The Cubbyhole - which used to be where Henrietta Hudson is - welcomes all persuasions. It isn't the least bit shy about it either as there's a Gents.

There's hardly enough room to swing a pussy in here and the black walls and decorations hanging from every inch of the low ceiling add to the warm, friendly vibe. Chinese paper lanterns, plastic fruit, fluffy toys, baubles and trinkets have all been tacked up.

Dotted around the bar are stools upholstered in vinyl depicting Warner Bros. favourites Daffy Duck, Porky Pig and serial cross-dresser Bugs Bunny. At the bar you can take your pick from Bass, Guinness and Stella (the drink, not the chick) on tap, and bottles of Bud, Becks, Corona and Amstel.

Local takeaways will deliver to the 'Hole and all the menus are kept behind the bar.

After dinner snaffle a handful of free popcorn and feed dollar bills into the excellent jukebox.

The Police's "Every Little Thing She Does Is Magic" gets the lasses up dancing, while "Fat Bottomed Girls" - Queen's ode to well-upholstered ladies - is guaranteed to raise eyebrows and smiles.

Dublin 6

Take me to: 575 Hudson St
(between W. 11th St and Bank St)

THEY say the Guinness is better in Dublin - and they're right. Dublin 6, which is to a post code in the Irish capital, has won awards for its black stuff. But here's a trade secret: Guinness is the same the world over, it's just a matter of how fresh the barrel is and how clean your pipes are.

And owner Jason O'Brien has taken great pride in his pipes since opening day in October 2002. If you're expecting the whole Irish pub-in-a-box thing of neon shamrocks and Van Morrison, then you're in the wrong part of town as it wouldn't last five minutes in the West Village.

Dublin 6 is a dark-red drinking den and restaurant. You wouldn't get the Pig & Whistle serving appetisers of roasted pear and goat cheese salad, followed by pan-seared organic king salmon. And they probably wouldn't let you play Connect 4 either, let alone lend you one from the collection behind the bar. True story, just ask for a box.

The walls are lined with photos of bons vivants from back home in Dublin 6, including a poor lad who's, hopefully, spewed on himself before passing out.

Curtains can be drawn across the bottom of the bar for private parties, but the area is mostly filled with groups of chums enjoying each other's company.

There's draught Boddies, Stella, Sam Adams lager and Kronenbourg; just shy of 40 bottles to choose from, with brews from Jamaica, Belgium, Germany, Holland and Oz, plus wine and champers.

Employees Only

Take me to: 510 Hudson St (at Christopher St)

A SIGN behind the bar warns: "Beware pickpockets and loose women". But if you need advice on who to avoid you'd be better off consulting the tarot card reader in the window. And after a quick shuffle of her deck she'll tell you your future involves drinking perfectly-mixed cocktails in one of the city's best lounges.

You'd need to be psychic to find this place as there's only a small awning with the stylish EO logo to tell you it's there. Owned and run by five professional bartenders named Jason, Dushan, Bill, Igor and Henry, the place is already super-famous across New York, despite only opening in late 2004.

Before the lads took over it was an Italian restaurant, but they gutted it and refitted it in the style of a classic NYC Prohibition-era speakeasy: only the restaurant's marble floor survived.

As you'd expect the drinks menu is extensive and they'll gladly mix you anything you want. So ask one of these jacketed pros for a Mata Hari - Courvoisier VS shaken with chai-infused vermouth and fresh squeezed pomegranate juice; or a Ruby Tuesday - Wild Turkey rye shaken with benedictine, lemon juice and pureed black cherries.

And the name? The West Village is crammed with restaurants and a lot of the staff pop in for a drink after they've closed up.

Gaslight

Take me to: 400 W. 14th St (at 9th Ave)

TO MERE mortals acres of the Meatpacking are out of bounds. If your name's not in big letters at the top of a movie poster, or you're not due to inherit a load of hotels, it's going to be an early night.

But let Lindsay and Paris have their cat fights on the other side of the velvet rope at whatever the hangout de jour is; we'll stick to brushing past Gaslight's velvety drapes.

Opened in October 1996, this wide open space resembles a Victorian parlour, the impression starting with the cobbles out on 9th Ave. There's the curtains and dark wood; the old mirrors and antique, high-backed chairs; the gas lamps and miniature street lamp on the bar.

One big room with a varnished wood floor is populated with well-worn furniture, several of the seatees looking like they escaped from M&S circa 1985. At weekends it's standing room only as the place gets packed with the friendly, unpretentious and not-so-shatteringly-fabulous denizens of the Meatpacking. Tues-Sat from 10pm there's a DJ, but the very with-it soundtrack tends to be disco-loud.

Weekday professionals in their Hilfiger shirts give way to cats in Converse All Stars at weekends. Gaslight's French windows are opened when the weather's warm and the fake-log gas fire's turned on when it's not. Once the door admission supervisors arrive you will get asked for ID, and groups of lads will get knocked back.

Henrietta Hudson Bar & Girl

Take me to: 438 Hudson St
(at Morton St)

IS IT hot in here or is it the girls? The Big Apple's gay guy scene may be huge but, apart from this place, scissor sisters in the 212 nabe are pretty much doing it for themselves.

Equal rights for women hasn't reached NYC's nightlife yet and that's fine with owner Lisa Cannistraci as it means her bar is always brimming with saucy minxes in the 20-40 bracket. If matronly librarians float your boat then try your luck in Barnes & Noble, because the chicks in here are hotter than July.

Henrietta's is split into two rooms; the first is exposed brick and dark wood with a cool metal-fronted bar and a DJ booth, plus a well-greased dancing pole in the window. Go through the doors into Room No2 and shoot some pool, sit and chat by the bar, watch pop videos or The L Word on DVD; or just sink your teeth into the eye candy.

DJs spin tunes every night and go-go girls entertain during Inferno on Saturdays. And there's no rest for the wicked as the temperature really rises on Sunday for the busiest night of the week. It all makes the pool tournament on Monday night seem a bit tame.

The bar, which was previously fellow lesbian hangout The Cubbyhole, is three blocks from the Henry Hudson River and Lisa simply feminised the name.

And the name isn't a typo: she meant it to say Bar & Girl.

Hudson Bar & Books

Take me to: 636 Hudson St
(at Horatio St)

"**NO MR** Bond, I expect you to order a single malt." Hudson B&B has styled itself more on the coolness of Connery than the suaveness of Moore, and even has a full set of 007 videos for your perusal.

The wood panelling gives this tiny lounge the look of a select gentlemen's club, while the colour of the ceiling tells you you're in one of the few bars in Manhattan where you can still legally light up.

Hudson's opened in 1990 as the city's first dedicated cigar bar. Cigars are the preferred weapon of choice, although you can happily puff away on your B&H if you like. Customers can smoke their own or sample a non-Cuban from the bar's stock.

When you order a cigar you'll be presented with a cutter, a candle, wooden lighters and a glass of water to snuff out the lighter, all on a metal tray - to which the cutter is chained.

Don't expect a cold Bud in here. This is strictly for the whisky and cocktail crowd and has a huge selection of malts, many of them older than the bartenders. The extra-special stuff is in a glass case behind the brass-topped bar, just by the pic of the toupee-wearing Sir Sean pouring himself a large one. Shaken, not stirred.

Once you sit by the fire in the library, armed with a leather-bound book and a single malt, talk of Pussy Galore, firing servants and bagging grouse will just trip off the tongue.

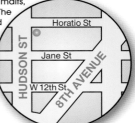

Plunge

Take me to: Hotel Gansevoort, 18 9th Ave (at 13th St)

YOU can only actually take the plunge if you've got a room key as the pool at this rooftop bar is guests only. But baby, who wants to be seen in their Speedos at the hippest scene in town?

Everyone from suits, trendies and celebs takes the lift to the 15th-floor penthouse on the ultra-cool Hotel Gansevoort. Exit the elevator and you'll enter a stunning lounge that's furnished with red, brown, and black leather sofas, ottomans and day beds. Tall palms in stone pots help keep things as cool as the soundtrack.

On the terrace there's more greenery in the shape of low hedges and neatly-clipped bushes. Wooden benches and loungers with plump cushions are all around. Smoking is allowed outside and the grey-metal Smokers Outposts are there for you to stub out your dimps.

The actual bar sits under a glass-covered terrace that looks like a big greenhouse and is furnished with low stools and tables. Entrance to the pool is also through this area.

It's plastic glasses only up here and they don't serve bottles as they don't want plebs launching their empties on to the Meatpacking's cobbles. On tap there's just Stella, Amstel Light and Heineken. Drinks aren't cheap and aren't a pint.

But there is the fantastically-named Tequila Mockingbird, a cocktail made from Jose Cuervo, fresh lemon, lime juice, and orange and cranberry juice.

AT STONEWALL PLACE

STONEWALL INN
SITE OF THE STONEWALL RIOTS
JUNE 27-29, 1969
BIRTH OF THE MODERN
LIBERATION

The Stonewall Inn

Take me to: 53 Christopher St (between Waverley Place & 7th Ave South)

THE Village People advised certain young men who didn't fancy a life on the ocean waves to "Go West". So if you're that way inclined head to the West Village for an encounter with the history books.

This is where it all started as Gay Liberation was born during the Stonewall Riots of June 27-29, 1969. And while your map will say you're on Christopher St, the street signs will proclaim it's actually Stonewall Place as it was renamed in honour of its pioneering tenant.

Stonewall is a gay, neighbourhood dive bar that's badly in need of a woman's touch; but you don't come here to discuss the curtains, which is just as well as they're Bet Lynch-esque leopard print.

The floor's wood, there's a pool table, no draught beer and a little 1970s-style seated area with mirrored walls above stripey seats. There's no drinks menu and just Bud, Bud Light, Heineken and Corona in bottles, along with various spirits. Upstairs is a party room where DJs spin tunes for you to groove to under the glitter ball.

During the afternoon the place has the feel of a local, if you'll pardon the expression. Not everyone's gay and all ages are covered. Most nights have a theme with Monday's Touch billed as "NYC's hottest hip-hop party"; while go-go boyz liven up Uncut on Fridays. Some nights have a small cover charge.

The Christopher St door closes at 10pm and the Seventh Ave entrance is used.

The White Horse Tavern

Take me to: 567 Hudson St (at 11th St)

DYLAN THOMAS drank his last in here. Legend has it the thirsty Welsh playwright sank 18 straight whiskies straight before declaring it a record, staggering into the street, falling arse over tit and then dying in St Vincent's hospital a few days later. As the bartender admitted: "It's not a happy story, but it put us on the map."

Occupying a corner spot in the West Village, this pub is popular with the brunch and lunch crowd and has seating outside, which gets full in warmer months. Inside is a roomy old bar manned by kindly staff who are only too happy to switch either of the two teles over to the golf, baseball, or horses of various hues if what's on isn't to your liking.

This front bar has tables and chairs under the windows and plenty of room for standing. The bar leads into two separate dining areas; the first with tables, the second with booths and the kitchen, and all with dark wood walls.

Choose from Newcy Brown, Stella, Guinness and White Horse ale on tap, or bottles of Woodpecker, Budweiser and Heineken.

The walls in the Gents owe more to Dylan of Bob fame than Thomas, as punters try their best to be profound.

Remarks are regularly cleaned off but we hope the fella who penned "There is good and evil" bought a drink for the bloke whose scrawled retort was "Evel Knievel is good".

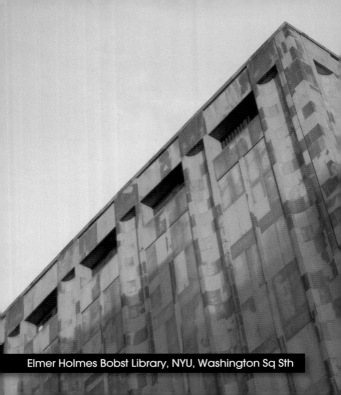

Elmer Holmes Bobst Library, NYU, Washington Sq Sth

Greenwich Village
& NoHo

Madame X

Take me to: 94 W. Houston St
(between La Guardia Place & Thompson St)

IF YOU'RE looking to inject a sexy little something into your date then this crimson-lit boudoir will put lead in your pencil, hair on your chest and a smile on the faces of you and the lady or gent on your arm.

Down the steps off the street you'll be enticed by subdued lighting, crushed velvet and leopard print, seductive seating and a surprising amount of singles of all persuasions.

Opened by Mimi Dimur and Amy McCloskey in 1997, Madame X is styled on a bordello. Mimi, who died in 2001, was French and wanted it to look like a sexy whorehouse. The name was chosen for its mystery. The girls later learned it was a famous painting by John Singer Sargent - a print of which now hangs on the stairs - and a film starring Lana Turner and John "Hello, Angels!" Forsyth.

There are no draught beers and just the likes of Corona, Guinness, Stella and Amstel Light in bottles. The bar leads into the lounge, where couples go to get to know each other better over the mismatched furniture and low sofas. And head for the door with the pouting lips if you fancy a fag in the smokers' garden.

The upstairs bar and atrium are decked out in the same style and open when it's lively or for a private party.

Amy specialises in Hen Nights, runs dating games for singles and classes in classic striptease. And her Anti-Super Bowl party is now legendary. Ooh-la-la!

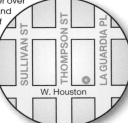

Marion's

Take me to: 354 Bowery
(between Great Jones & E. 4th Sts)

THIS camp cocktail lounge has been a New York institute since 1950 - including the 17 years it didn't exist. It's a story of Cold War shenanigans, and a beautiful and determined woman. Are you sitting comfortably...

Marion Nagy fled Stalinist Budapest just after the Second World War. As a member of the Hungarian Swim Team she attended the World Peace Games in Paris, where she executed her crafty plan to flee. She became a high-couture model, but as her career in France took off she feared her fame would alert the Reds back home so she did a runner again, this time to NYC, and set up her lounge.

Frequented by the likes of JFK and Sinatra, Marion's was the place to be until she closed it in 1973 to look after her three young boys. But in 1990 her son, Richard Bach, rebuilt the place using old snapshots.

And it's exactly as she would have remembered it, with purple walls and 1950s vinyl stools. Clients range from 20s-60s and some of the old timers used to pop in when Marion ran things.

It's big on food and has plenty of room for dining. As for cocktails, there's Piper's Pink Panty Pulldown, Sex With Your Ex and the house special The Marion; a dry Stoli gibson up with an olive.

Back in her heyday Marion had celebs sign plates for the walls, but they all went missing a long time ago. There are still plates on display - but the biggest names up there now are Moby and Geri Halliwell.

Peculier Pub

Take me to: 145 Bleecker St
(between Thompson St & La Guardia Place)

THERE'S nothing peculiar about the name of this Greenwich Village dive, no matter what the locals might say. Us Brits know it's named after a famous beer from these isles, don't we? Well, we do now.

A beer drinker's paradise and the perfect place to do the "Who's throwing beer mats?" gag, the Peculier Pub is popular with NYU students attracted by the selection and prices - and people who like beer.

There are over 500 bottles and two dozen brews on tap. Add to this a selection of martinis, wines, frozen margaritas, cocktails and beer-tails, and you'll appreciate it's not for the lily-livered.

Sitting under a saggy metal ceiling are worn wooden pews and tables, all with names and messages of undying love carved, felt-tipped and scorched into them. The PP's almost as big on chat as it is beer and small talk and raucous badinage are encouraged.

Brick walls are covered with mirrors and neon signs, while at the bottom end of the bar by the toilets are colourful bottle-top mosaics, including one of King Tut.

The boring will plump for a Mackeson but the adventurous might try Scotland's Kalpi Seaweed Ale. Many beers on the menu have their alcohol content listed, as well as the size of the bottle they come in.

It's always wise to get some food inside you before you have a skinful and the pub offers a choice of "Old Standbys" like curly fries, pizzas and sarnies.

Swift Hibernian Lounge

Take me to: 34 E. 4th St (between Bowery and Lafayette)

IF YOU met three Irish sisters you'd want them to look like The Corrs and not any of The Nolans. Face it, you'd rather snog the bloke in The Corrs than The Nolans. Along with Puck Fair and Ulysses', Swift makes up a Gaelic sisterhood every bit as cheeky as the raven-haired temptresses.

Named after Gulliver's Travels author Jonathan, the wall facing the curved wooden bar is decorated with murals showing scenes from his life and works. One depicts the ghost of a girl haunting her father in Dublin's Marsh's Library. Before topping herself she left a note for her lover in a book, but he never found it. The Library is next to St Patrick's Cathedral where Swift was Dean and where his body now lies.

Swift's second room is kitted out with wooden benches, tables and pews. A long table you can easily cram 20 people round occupies the middle of the room. Every Tuesday there's a traditional seisiun in here, while Thursday to Saturday DJs survey their flock from a pulpit which was imported from Ireland.

The bar's well stocked with the draughts and bottles listed on blackboards. Beers from the tap are served in 20oz pints and non-Imperial glasses for Belgian brews.

Swift's "Hearty Fare" includes stuffed spuds, soup, bangers 'n mash and Dollar Dogs, which speak for themselves.

The owners also run the Swift Shuttle and seven days a week they'll happily bus you between their three boozers FOC.

Temple Bar

Take me to: 332 Lafayette St
(between Bleecker & Houston Sts)

IF YOU want to get in the mood for some loving then this sexy little spot will soon have you in a lather. You just know you're in for a saucy-kinda night when you walk up to a place and can't see in. Oh yes, the curtains are always drawn at the Temple Bar.

Step past the lizards on the outside wall and into a lounge with dark wood and black décor, lowest-of-the-low-level lighting, sexy waitresses in strappy LBDs (all with perfect posture), seating to get intimate on and more martinis than you can shake a certain well-known British secret agent at. Well there are 68 vodkas on the menu.

There's an extensive choice of Italian aperitifs, cocktails and special martinis, and staff can whip you up an Espresso Martini from vodka, espresso and espresso liquer; or a Flirtini: vodka, champagne, Cointreau and pineapple juice.

Saddo singles will nab a retro 1950s-style bar stool and tuck into the free olives and popcorn, but couples will head to the lounge, although the soundtrack can get in the way of whispered sweet nothings.

Drinks are a tad pricey and there's nine bottled beers to choose from, including Czechvar, Sapporo and Grolsch. But you didn't come in for a pint and some nuts.

The Temple Bar is strictly lovers only necking licentious libations, and a cosy canoodle a deux will definitely leave you feeling stirred, not shaken.

In Loving Memory of
POPE
John Paul
II

by: CHICO
PETE
2005

Born: 1920
Died: April 2 2005

Pope John Paul II mural, E. Houston St (at Ave B)

5

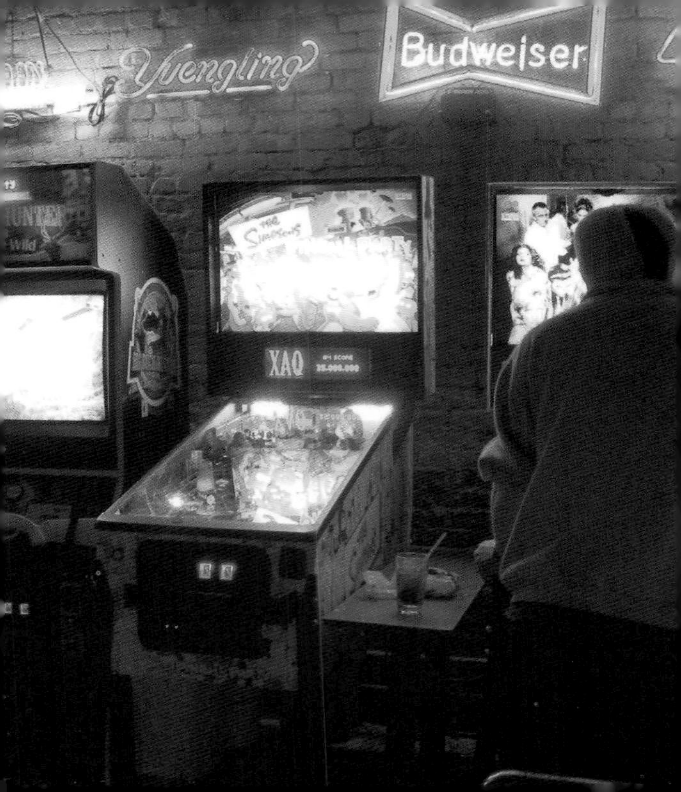
Yuengling
Budweiser
XAQ

Ace Bar

Take me to: 531 E. 5th St
(between Aves A & B)

WOW! Rock 'n roll! And lunchboxes. Cold beer, pool, darts, staff with 'tude, a kick-ass jukebox, and a collection of over 100 metal lunchboxes all combine to make this dive bar a cool East Village hangout.

There's plenty of room in the Ace, which is darker than one of spades. At the authentically-sticky bar you can choose from a dozen draught beers like Strongbow, Guinness and Boddies, or bottles of Newcy Brown, Corona and Budweiser.

The Ace used to be Goth hangout The Mission until 1993 when it was decided to liven up the miserable, mascara-wearing buggers. The new owners also amalgamated their lunchbox collections and lovingly displayed them in three floor-to-ceiling glass cases. All originals, there's Inch High Private Eye, The Hair Bear Bunch, Six Million Dollar Man and The Bionic Woman; and Barry Gibb sporting a gorgeous gold-towelling tracky top.

Down in the large games room at the back there's ample standing room and red vinyl seating for you to relax on until it's your turn on either of the pool tables. Or you may decide to chuck some arrows at the twin dartboards.

Ace is open 12/7 every day and if you feel yourself flagging then get a few E numbers down you with a handful of Skittles from the dispenser, which takes quarters.

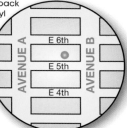

Angel's Share

Take me to: 8 Stuyvesant St
(between 3rd Ave & 9th St)

NEW YORK'S most romantic-sounding bar is also one of its strictest. No more than four to a group, no standing and no shouting or screaming. And you must wait to be seated, don't just blunder in and pull up a pew. Commit any of these crimes and you'll be out. Seriously. But good behaviour is rewarded with some of the city's best cocktails.

This Japanese lounge is a bugger to find and is definitely one of the city's best-kept secrets, which helps keep the out riff-raff. Head through the door under the canopy and up the stairs to Japanese restaurant Village Yoko Cho. Once inside look for the unmarked door, walk in and wait.

The heavenly little hide-out gets its name from the term given to the amount of spirit that evaporates from warehoused barrels. The no-more-than-four rule is spot on as Angel's Share is best experienced with that certain special someone coz it's right off the romance-ometer.

Above the bar is a mural of cherubs on the lash, while through a curtain at the end of the bar is an intimate second room. Cool jazz provides the soundtrack, which is low enough so you won't break any rules by shouting. There's also a menu of tasty titbits like fresh raw oyster and Japanese satay assortment.

The strictness of the place may give some brewer's droop but your date will think you're Heaven sent.

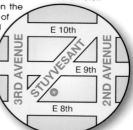

Burp Castle

Take me to: 41 E. 7th St
(between 2nd & 3rd Aves)

SOLVING murders can be thirsty work and after a hard day's sleuthing Cadfael would feel right at home here - because the pumps are manned by monks. Well, everywhere needs a gimmick.

The Burp Castle has another Unique Selling Point and that's its choice of 250 brews, with the Friar Tuck dopplegangers only too glad to let you have a sip of whatever it is you can't make your mind up about.

There's no cold Buds here and the beers constantly change. Throw in 30 different bottles and you'll find something to suit every liver.

It's always lively, despite the Gregorian Chants on the stereo, and come Oktoberfest the place sways to the sound of the polka. The pumps take on a Germanic theme and brews include Fatherland faves Ramstein, Bitburger and Hofbrau.

During Oktoberfest you can help yourself to free German sausage, the rest of the year you'll be offered Belgian fries on Mondays and Wednesdays. Menus for local restaurants are on hand and you can have your fried tuck delivered to your high stool or the 12-seater garden out front.

The dark-wood interior adds to the gothic air and the walls are covered with murals of shipwrecked, carousing monks. Signs around the walls warn "No loud talking allowed - whispers only", but with so many tasty brews, tongues tend to get a little loose.

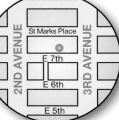

KGB Bar

Take me to: 85 E. 4th St
(between Bowery & 2nd Ave)

WE'RE sure Comrades Lenin and Brezhnev wouldn't approve of you drinking Budweiser but they've been dead years so who cares.

The beer's as Cold as the War once was in this former front for the Ukrainian Communist Party which masqueraded as a Ukrainian Men's Club for over 40 years. The Feds would have been kept busy by this place down the years as, back in the 1920s, it was a speakeasy before becoming a Commie HQ.

But in 1993 Denis Woychuk, whose papa was a former member, turned this small, first-floor parlour in an East Village redbrick into a bar and called it the Kraine Gallery & Bar - KGB for short. He kept all the original fixtures and fittings like the oak bar, leaded-glass panels and USSR paraphernalia, including photos of Soviet big cheeses and the Hammer and Sickle flag behind the bar. If there's ever a Sputnik on eBay the place'll be complete.

You can still sample Uncle Nikolai's vodka if you like, or you can plump for Baltika, Bud, Beck's and Corona in bottles.

In keeping with its secretive past, KGB is home to New York's underground poets and literati and has readings three nights a week.

KGB has a theatre above and below and caters to the cerebral and avant-garde amongst us. It may not be to everyone's taste, but neither's caviar.

McSorley's

Take me to: 15 E. 7th St (between 2nd & 3rd Aves)

IF EVER Worzel Gummidge and Albert Steptoe got on Changing Rooms this would be the finished product. You have to experience McSorley's to believe it - and appreciate it.

Anything that can be nailed, glued, hung, tacked or taped to the walls has been. Faded, dust-covered pictures, ornaments and Kennedy Clan paraphernalia; it's all here. The place reeks of hops, there's sawdust on the floor and you can have any beer you like as long as it's the incredibly moreish McSorley's light or dark.

Over 150 years old, this Irish pub is jumping every night with regulars, tourists and the 4x4 crew. The tables look as if they've been there since Day One and are scarred with decades of carvings.

It also looks like the only things that get cleaned are the glasses and the pipes, but there's a very good reason why the light fitting over the bar has wishbones hanging from it - and almost 90 years of dust.

Before many of his regulars went off to serve with the Fighting 69th in the First World War, owner Bill McSorley cooked each of them a turkey dinner.

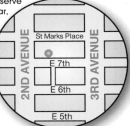

Once they'd cleaned their plates, the lads hung their bird's wishbone on the light, where they stayed until their return. The bones still hanging there belong to the brave men who fell in battle.

Now isn't that a story worth raising a glass to?

Nevada Smith's

Take me to: 74 3rd Ave (between 11th & 12th Sts)

THE days of phoning home to find out if your team's won, lost or drawn are over. If you're into association football and nylon replica shirts, then this is the place to be.

Nevada Smith's is named after a little-known Steve McQueen western and its black walls are about as interesting to look at. If there's no football on, forget it, but once the ref's blown his whistle this place throbs with lust for the Beautiful Game. There's more passion in here than a roasting session at The Grosvenor.

Everything from the Carling Cup to Serie A via the Championship and World Cup qualifiers is shown live. The fun starts at 7am on Saturdays with the early Premiership game, while Sundays are ram-packed as the various TVs show action from around Europe. But things really get lively when Manchester United are on telly.

Nevada Smith's is home to the New York Reds and a shrine to the Evil Empire. Wear you shirt on game day - regardless of your team - and relive the days of the terraces as the partisan atmosphere gets a grip on you and the chants start flying.

United fans will soak it all up and bathe in the bright-red glow. Non-Reds might feel like taking a shower.

Prawn sandwiches aren't on the menu but you can buy an hot pie at half-time.

Just remember, there is a cover charge for the football as it's supplied by Setanta.

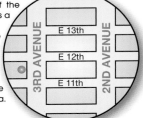

The Sunburnt Cow

Take me to: 137 Ave C
(between 8th & 9th Sts)

THE bar is named in memory of Bessie, Aussie owner Heathe St Clair's childhood pet cow; a bovine that actually did get sunburnt during a heat wave in 1972. And then ended up on the family's barbie.

Heathe has kept the lighting low with the only bright spots provided by candles and illuminated squares under the bar, which is built from oil drums. The walls are bare brick and rough plaster while the garden out back - no pun intended - is designed to look like a cave with rough rock walls. It's also open to the elements as there's no roof, just a canopy of trees that lean over from La Plaza Cultural next door.

Our Antipodean pals like a drop of the amber nectar although you won't find Fosters here. You can buy Guinness, Amstel and Heineken by the pint, along with imported Aussie and Kiwi beers. Or try a Whinging Pom, a cocktail made from muddled orange, mint, sugar, pomegranate juice and Tanqueray.

Reminders of Bessie are everywhere and range from multi-coloured cow-print stools, to pictures of cows and the Bessie Sandwich. Heathe's a proud Aussie and serves a free Vegemite sandwich with every brunch.

The Sunburnt Cow has many unique selling points but the vodka-based Moo Juices are a work of genius. All served in babies' bottles, they come complete with a rubber teat to suckle on.

It's what Bessie would have wanted.

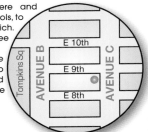

The Telephone Bar & Grill

Take me to: 149 2nd Ave
(between 9th & 10th Sts)

A REGULAR slice of 'ome this is and make no mistake, guv'nor. You'll think you're back in Blighty when you clap your minces on the three red phone boxes on the street. And they all work.

Large and well-lit, the bar is lined with stools while the rest of the front room is given over to tables for diners. At the back there's a quieter, darker room that comes with its own fire and is used for parties, live music and film nights.

An East Village attraction since 1988, the Telephone Bar & Grill has set its stall out in the style of Del Boy. It offers Newcastle Brown, London Pride, Strongbow, Stella and Boddies on tap, and can also serve you a bottle of Monty Python's Holy Ail, which is "Tempered over burning witches".

If you're feeling peckish why not try their Ploughman's Lunch (complete with Branston), bangers and mash, shepherd's pie, or an Irish Breakfast, which is the same as its English rival minus the fried bread.

And if that doesn't have you phoning your mum in tears then their fish and chips will. Served in newspaper, they were voted the best in New York City in 2002 and are available with lashings of HP Sauce!

Most places have queues for the toilets but this place has one stretching from the phone boxes as, late on, the worse-for-wear think they can get out that way.

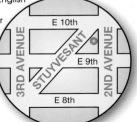

Velvet Cigars

Take me to: 80 E. 7th St
(between 1st & 2nd Aves)

THIS tiny cigar lounge only got its booze licence at the turn of 2006. Before that the strongest thing you could buy - apart from a Robusto Gorda - was Sprite, although you could bring your own bottle.

Now you can nurse a bottle of Pilsner Urquell, Magic Hat or Hoegaarden; a glass of Zinfandel, Cabernet Sauvignon or Chianti; or even a 40-year-old tawny Port, white wine and champers.

Velvet's stock of Dominican cigars starts at less than $10 and the mild, medium and full-bodied smokes range in size from panatellas to Churchills. It gets its fair share of the fairer sex and the sambuca, mint and cherry-flavoured stogies are a big hit with the girls.

With only six chairs and five stools to sit on you've got to be quicker than a German hunting sun loungers in Benidorm to get a seat. There is room to stand and the wood panelling - which covers the wall to chest height - has a ledge for ashtrays and glasses.

Cigarette smoking is outlawed in all but a few New York night spots but there's nothing more civilised than relaxing with a good cigar, a stiff drink and good company while listening to The Kinks and The Beatles.

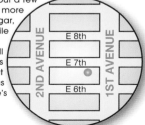

Crimson velvet curtains frame the small window and a wooden Indian stands guard by the door, keeping an eye out for celebs. The bootylicious Beyonce has been spotted on the street, though she's yet to be seen sucking on a Churchill.

Zum Schneider

Take me to: 107 Ave C
(at 7th St)

MANY a tipsy reveller has greeted Herr Schneider with a friendly "Hiya Zum!". He'll smile and answer them, even though it's not his name. It's not even his nickname. For the record, he's a Sylvester and Zum is the same as Chez for French restaurants and means "to" or "at".

Zum Schneider opened in August 2000 because Sylvester was homesick, missed the Bavarian craic and couldn't get decent beer in New York. The only fakes in here are the concrete trees and plastic ivy wrapped around them. All his staff speak German, the drinks come in steins and you can't have ice coz that's not the Bavarian way.

Tables, chairs and benches of various shapes and sizes cover the bare concrete floor and the air is always thick with conversation.

The 11 draught beers consist of wheat, pilsener, lager, dark and doppelbeck, and amber and are poured in small, medium and large. There's also seven bottles, plus Gerolsteiner Mineralwasser.

Sylvester's menu covers everything from a plate of traditional German cold cuts and cheeses, weiner schnitzel, Bavarian meatball soup and side orders of sauerkraut.

The chap in the painting, who looks like he's just stepped out of a Flashman novel, is King Ludwig II von Bayern (1845-1886), who founded Schloss Neuschwanstein. And try saying that after a skinful of Spaten Optimator.

Achtung baby.

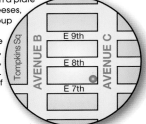

Chelsea Hotel, 222 W. 23rd St

HOTEL
CHELSEA

6

Barracuda

Take me to: 275 W. 22nd St (between 7th & 8th Aves)

AN INTERIOR straight out of Elle Décor and hot-as-hell guys await you in this hip gay bar with an anonymous-looking front door.

Barracuda is all designer furniture, black paint, dark wood and sophistication. And eye candy in the 20-40 age bracket.

The back-lit bar has two mini DVD players showing video compilations, the gist of which seem to be buffed blokes running about with nothing on. Classic Sputnik lights hang from the ceiling, while elegant lamps grace the two high tables in the front bar. And the décor in the back room would blow the budget for three series of Changing Rooms.

Enter a short passage, pass the DJ booth, side step the pool table and you're in the cabaret room. Midnight Sunday to Thursday there's a drag show on stage, with fag hags Eartha Kitt, Tammy Faye Baker and Tonya Harding known to call in for a peek.

The ultra-desirable De Sede leather seating bends both ways, somewhat inappropriately. But along with the moody lighting it's perfect for chatting up whichever non-straight guy has caught your queer eye.

Early doors the music comes from an iPod but a DJ takes control every night at 10pm and teases you with 80s synth-pop before making it more dancey.

At the bar there's a small selection of bottles including Perrier, Bud, Heineken and Corona and a wide range of spirits.

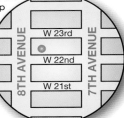

Brite Bar

Take me to: 297 10th Ave (at 27th St)

FAMED for its cross-town view of the Empire State Building, this bar in the hugely-gay Chelsea area gets its name from the kids' Lite Brite game.

During the summer the trees in Chelsea Park across the street do their best to partially block the view of the ESB but come the winter the world's most famous skyscraper is visible in all her glory. And you'll also know when it's midnight as that's when they turn her lights off.

The seating is cool, low and chat-friendly and there's a curved suede banquette at the bottom of this joint, which is equipped with plenty of standing room and DJs. And no, that girl in the toilet queue isn't wearing the same top as you, it's a mirrored door.

Cute bartenders of both sexes will serve you Brite's signature cocktail, the Fother Mucker, Hoegaarden, O'Hara's Irish Stout or Sam Adams on draught, and Newcastle Brown, Stella and Bud in bottles. There's also plenty of champers chilling and a selection of wines.

Formerly an arcade game repair shop, the Brite Bar is a popular jump-off point for Chelsea clubbers. Punters generally drop by early doors before hitting the town and then return just before 3am after going a few rounds.

But as the sign warns: "We're sorry you didn't get into "that club" . . . please don't bitch about it here. Have fun!".

So if you're desperate to be "scene", head for somewhere with a velvet rope.

Flatiron Lounge

Take me to: 37 W. 19th St (between 5th & 6th Aves)

NEVER mix your drinks - get an expert to do it instead. And with super-mixtress Julie Reiner in attendance you're in very good hands. Julie and her co-owners opened this beauty in June 2003 but you'll swear blind it's 1923 once inside.

Through the door and past the babelicious greeter girl there lies a classic New York Art Deco lounge, into which you're lured through an arched, candle-lit hallway.

The lighting's low, the music's swingin' and the mood is intimate. There are cosy little tables for couples and a red leather banquette along one wall. Above that is a stunning arrangement of cobalt glass tiles from the 1920s.

If you're feeling unadventurous sit at the bar and swig from a bottle of Heineken or Amstel Light, or a pint of Guinness or Stella. But the lads and lasses behind the 30ft-long bar that used to grace the Manhattan Ballroom way back when weren't hired because they can pull a decent pint of Boddies.

La Reiner's menu evokes the bygone days of the cocktail lounge - perfectly.

Try a Hotel Nacional Special (Cuba, circa 1933), which is billed as the perfect daiquiri. Or quench your thirst with a Persephone, a pomegranate martini named after the Queen of the Underworld. Just don't show us up by asking for a packet of crisps.

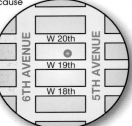

g lounge

Take me to: 225 W. 19th St (between 7th and 8th Aves)

WHICHEVER story you tell about how g got its name, just don't spell it with a capital letter. Some say the place is shaped like a g - it isn't. Or g for gay because it's a gay bar? Nope, so keep guessing.

Opened in 1997, g is - according to owner Michael McGrail - the city's original upscale gay lounge and the birthplace of the Frozen Cosmo. Michael wanted a place where gay men could meet their straight pals without feeling embarrassed by its sleaziness; and vice versa.

After work the place fills up nicely as hipsters and smart professionals of all persuasions chatter away before the disco bunnies turn up.

Dominated by the arched window on W. 19th St, the front section and bar resemble a gay Ikea with their pale wood and brushed metal. Faux leather sofas and ottomans - which are persimmon and pistachio - add splashes of colour. The curves of the metal bar will guide you to the semi-circular alcove where the acoustics make it perfect for an intimate natter.

Punters range from 20s-50s with the crowd getting younger as the night gets older. g prides itself on its cocktails, which change with the seasons, and the Jingle Bell Rocks, made from sweet blackberry Black Haus peppered with spicy Southern Comfort, will make any Yuletide gay.

And you never know, after you've hit g once, it could just become your most-favourite spot.

GYM Sports Bar

Take me to: 167 8TH AVE (between 18th and 19th Sts)

WHAT could be more relaxing than having a few beers, some popcorn and shooting the breeze and some pool with the lads? Well until March 2005 gay New Yorkers might have felt uneasy sitting in a regular sports bar and enduring comments about taking one for the team. But then along came GYM.

The Apple's only gay sports bar is the brainchild of Rick Schmutzler, a 6ft 4in, 17st former American footballer, who also happens to like men. And that's **gay** sports bar, not **gay-sports** bar.

GYM is a large, brickwalled, open space with a pool table, sofas and teles showing live sport. As it's co-owner Rick's gaff, it's Rick's rules and he will never allow a cover charge, go-go boys or porn in GYM. True, on busy nights there's more blokes checking each other out than what's on the box but you workout in a gym, right?

On tap you can pick from Stella, Sam Adams and Bud, while in cans you'll find Guinness Draught and bottles of Grolsch, Newcastle Brown, Corona, Rolling Rock and Woodpecker. And they don't serve aftershave when the rugby's on.

Regulars are aged between 20-60, with the majority early-30s to late-40s. Staff run the gamut of gym bunny to leather daddy and there's a few straight 'tenders thrown into the mix. Early on they play an eclectic mix of tunes before the DJs take control Thursday to Sunday.

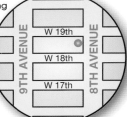

The Half King

Take me to: 505 W. 23rd St (between 10th & 11th Aves)

THE cosy little suntrap out back is a dead ringer for one of those beer gardens where as a kid, you'd get left with a bottle of Coke and those crisps with the little blue bag of salt. But now you're all grown up and can order Strongbow.

At night there's a waiting list for a table in the candle-lit garden and for the street-light-bathed area on the pavement out front, both of which are non-smoking.

This bustling Chelsea pub is named after the 18th Century Seneca chief Tanaghrisson, who had dealings with George Washington, and is co-owned by Sebastian Junger, author of "A Perfect Storm".

The staff are young, tattooed and hip but the customers are a mix of young and arty, old and arty, blue-collar hard hats, gay and straight. At the long, well-worn bar you can choose from 10 draughts, including Guinness, Stella and Newcy Brown, or Bud, Corona and Rolling Rock in bottles.

There are five booths in the bar and a separate dining room with leather sofas and art exhibitions. Food is served from 9am-3.30am and the chef will rustle you up a breakfast with a pot or Earl Grey, fish and chips, a veggie burger or a slice of Jack Daniels Pecan Pie.

Sunday night there's free live music and on Mondays Seb gets novelists and poets in for readings.

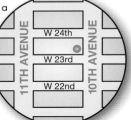

Serena

Take me to: Chelsea Hotel, 222 W. 23rd St (between 7th & 8th Aves)

THIS dark lounge lurks under the famously infamous Chelsea Hotel, where Dylan Thomas stayed before setting off to drown his whistle at the White Horse Tavern, and where Sid killed Nancy. Allegedly.

Head past the doorman at street level and descend into a place that reflects the hotel's decadent past. The walls are black and blood red, which is actually a Vicious pink up close but it's so dark in here they look crimson. And despite the three-watt bulbs and candles, the clientele still look young and groovy but not achingly-hip.

The actual bar occupies the middle of three rooms. The first can be closed off behind plush drapes for private functions and is decorated with black and white photos of celebs like Warhol and an Holiday-era Madge. The third is full of low tables, cubey cushions and sexy sofas.

Our heroin-addled Punk sweethearts even have a cocktail named after them. The Sid and Nancy is made from raspberry vodka, amaretto chambord, raspberry puree, fresh lime and soda water, served up.

DJs will happily spin old skool beats and they all know how to keep the music at a level that won't drown out the chit-chat.

The fact Nancy Spungen was only 20 when she checked out means nothing nowadays as you will get asked for ID by the guy up on the street. Quentin Crisp was once an hotel resident and the art-filled lobby is definitely worth a look.

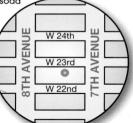

Trailer Park Lounge & Grill

Take me to: 271 W. 23rd St (between 7th & 8th Aves)

DOLLY PARTON, Elvis Presley, Johnny Cash, Hank Williams - your boys took one helluva beating. If you like your food fried, your beer cold and your trash white, then look no further. You've got to be in for a wild ride in a joint that has half a caravan stuck on the wall, right?

The place is plastered with 1950s memorabilia, including original signs advertising 7-up, Coca-Cola and Ann Marie's Beauty Salon.

An old TV continuously shows movies and shows from 50 years ago and Elvis looks down on you from all four walls. The tables and chairs are straight out of Happy Days and there's even strategically-placed plastic privet hedges and palm trees. And the odd flamingo.

If The King were alive he'd make a B-line for this place and see if the tribute acts that occasionally entertain the masses do him justice. The impersonators' mug shots have a wall of their own, with this week's star atttraction getting the honour of the gold frame.

This Vegas indoors will sell you a Trailer Park Lounge temporary tattoo, a t-shirt and even knickers if you're all out of clean 'uns.

A margarita pitcher serves six and you can get Rolling Rock, Sam Adams and Miller Lite on draught. Bottles of Bud, Corona and cans of Pabst Blue Ribbon are kept on ice in a bath - that also has the top half of a shop dummy in it.

Grease is still the word and it's probably Grilled Fat Dogs or burgers you can smell.

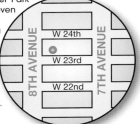

View from Empire State Building

Beauty Bar

Take me to: 231 E. 14th St (betwen 2nd & 3rd Aves)

LIBERACE didn't die - he moved to New York and opened a bar. OK, that's a lie but the late joanna-thumping queen would have adored the chandeliers in here. And he'd probably spend hours sitting under one of the original chrome hairdryers getting his pinkies manicured, which you can do Tuesday-Saturday evenings while sipping a Blue Rinse margarita.

Only in New York could a 1960s beauty salon be turned into one of the quirkiest, coolest and best-loved bars in town. The Beauty Bar has kept all its original fixtures and fittings. Along with the hairdryers, the walls are decked out with mirrors, ads and pictures of Ann-Margaret look-a-likes sporting what was the latest do. And shelves behind the bar display 40-year-old bottles of ointments, talc and Danderine shampoo.

Patrons range from hip 20-somethings to even-hipper pensioners, with many sporting vintage togs that have been in and out of fashion and are now in again. But you don't have to be a cool cat to feel at home here; this isn't the Meatpacking and the suits have come straight from the office, not the catwalk.

Some of the DJing can best be described as experimental but the decks by the door are manned every night.

It's all a bit creepy in a dead-mum, Norman Bates/Jimmy Saville kinda way but a visit to this unique haunt where Gramercy meets the East Village is a must.

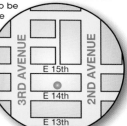

Old Town Bar & Grill

Take me to: 45 E. 18th St
(between Broadway & Park Ave South)

ONE of New York's finest-looking bars - literally. The mahogany and marble bar runs 55ft, almost the full length of the room, and is backed by huge bevel-edged mirrors with a 16ft-high tin ceiling above.

Opened in 1892 it's a classic saloon bar with a real lived-in look and a neon sign outside that used to feature on the opening titles to The Late Show with David Letterman.

Its interior also inspired the set for The Iceman Cometh and Madonna strutted along the bar in her video for Bad Girl.

The Old Town doesn't need a crowd to arrive to get things started as its local feel and clientele keep it ticking over. But you never know when an A-list celeb will drop in for a livener as Tom Cruise and Brad Pitt have previously propped up the bar. Regular Liam Neeson used to bring Natasha Richardson here when they were courting.

Try and bag one of the wooden booths and have a bite to eat. Some of them still have Prohibition-era storage spaces where booze was hastily stashed during a police raid. If the bar's full, head upstairs to the restaurant.

One huge turn off in the Old Town is anyone whose mobile is turned on. The bartenders made the news after they decided to ban them.

So if yours starts playing The Crazy Frog, you'll be told to go outside and won't get served until you've hung up.

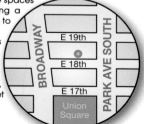

Pete's Tavern

Take me to: 129 E. 18th St (at Irving Place)

OPENED in 1864 during the Civil War, Pete's lays claim to the title of oldest original bar in NYC. Its saloon-style, rosewood bar and wood-panelled interior give it a cosy, inviting feel and make it a perfect place to stop and fend off the winter chills.

The joint stayed open during Prohibition by operating a flower stall out front to hide the goings on inside; and by fitting a getaway door out back for when The G Men decided to drop by unannounced.

Pete's draught range includes Guinness, Warsteiner, Stella, Pete's 1864 House Ale and even Double Diamond; bottles of Bud, St Pauli Girl and Woodchick cider are also available.

O. Henry wrote "The Craft of the Magi" sitting in one of Pete's booths back in 1905, with the aforementioned spot now bearing the author's name.

Above the booths are glass cases crammed full of knick-knacks and mementoes, while signed photos of celeb patrons adorn the walls.

The table cloths are paper but it beats trying to wash out all the pasta sauce that's spilled by diners in the backroom. The bar gets three-deep once the after-work crowd arrive and it also sees its fair share of tourists.

And the late JFK Jnr became a regular after seeing the picture of his mum and dad that hangs at the end of the bar.

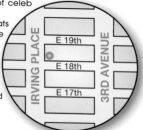

Empire State Building, view along W. 34th St

Bryant Park Café & Grill

Take me to: 25 W. 40th St
(between 5th & 6th Aves)

SLAP-BANG on 42nd St, despite its address, and tucked behind the city's Public Library is an indoor/outdoor, smoking/non-smoking people magnet in a park full of people.

The Café and Grill fills two blocks and consists of a downstairs, an upstairs and two outsides. If you want to be stuffy and sit inside admiring your jewellery then the Grill is for you. Here you'll find a marble-fronted bar that serves draught Wife Beater and Heineken, bottles of Bud Light, Becks and Grolsch and a wide range of wines and spirits.

Inside you can sit at the bar or dine at the tables. Outside a forest of umbrellas cover the dining area, with the garden terrace on the roof.

Smoking is allowed up there and it's a good place to sit, sip and inhale as you watch movies on the big screen in the Park during Mondays in the summer. This rooftop bar is, bizarrely, only open weekdays and the Café is sometimes closed for private parties.

While you're up there look down to your right and if you think the people by the green marquees are having more fun than you, it's time to visit the Café.

You can spark up wherever down here and smoke cigars at the bar after 2pm. The Café has a large dining area and plenty of room around its two bars.

And there's a certain Britishness about the whole place as they shut at 11pm when the park keepers lock up.

Cellar Bar

Take me to: The Bryant Park, 40 W. 40th St (between 5th & 6th Aves)

PRISONERS of cool will gladly take the long walk down the steps into this Gothic dungeon. Beneath the deeply-groovy Bryant Park hotel basque-clad waitresses do their best to keep the temperature up in this candle-lit lair; even if it's just the heat from the stare you'll get for ogling all the thigh they're flashing.

Enter the hotel lobby and head to the left, down the low flight of stone steps into the bar where vaulted ceilings, slate floors, pimply-leather seats and flickering candles await you.

You can get served at the bar or beckon one of the mini-skirted vamps, who'll turn up brandishing a bowl of Bombay Mix. There's low seating down the sides and high stools and tables in the middle of the room. At the bar there's space for about 10 bums on seats.

Cocktails are known as Flirtatious Fusions in here and all have names like Foreplay, Thai Me Up, Sake-2-Me and Porn Starr. But if you just want a beer it's still called Guinness, Sapporo, Stella or Bud Light.

It's a professional crowd with the punters getting more fabulous later on. After work it's suits, boots and Jimmy Choos as they unwind over a drink and a laid-back soundtrack. The velvet rope will also pop up outside late on at weekends.

Despite the waitresses' fetishtic air it's your wallet, not your arse, that might get spanked in here as it's a little bit pricey.

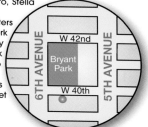

ESPN Zone

Take me to: 1472 Broadway, Times Sq (at 42nd St)

THAT new High Definition-ready plasma TV you've just shelled out on looks like a portable compared to the two 14ft, Hi-Def bad boys up on the first floor. Just think Comet - with cold beer and burgers.

If American sport is your thing and you haven't got a ticket then get in the Zone. Yes it's touristy and the busy shop can satisfy all your ESPN-goody needs - from t-shirts to martini glasses, bathmats to golf balls - but on a cold Sunday afternoon in winter this really is the only place to watch the NFL. Apart from Giants Stadium but that's over in Jersey.

Space is at a premium when pigskin's in season and they stand four deep at the 40ft-long bar in the first-floor Screening Room. This is where the action is and beers are served in chilled 25oz glass tankards, with Wife Beater, Bud Light, Sam Adams and Coors Light on offer.

Around the super screens are more teles, each tuned to a different channel and sport. The quieter Bristol Suite is next door and has the order of the day's NFL games below each TV.

Food is exactly what you'd expect, with artery-blocking steaks, buffalo wings, cheese burgers and fries alongside Caesar Salads that'd feed a legion.

Next to the shop on the ground floor is the Studio Grill, which always has a queue for tables. The second-floor Sports Arena arcade has a bar and is popular with harassed parents who dump the kids up there with a pocketful of quarters.

Flute Champagne Lounge

Take me to: 205 W. 54th St
(between Broadway and 7th Ave)

THIS civilised little hidey hole is an island of champagne-induced calm in Times Square's ocean of neon craziness.

Opened in 1997, Flute is housed in the former premises of notorious Prohibition speakeasy Club Intime; below street level, under the arch and down the steps. In honour of its past a bottle of Krug 1928 has been sealed in a glass case in the floor.

There are over 100 champagnes and sparkling wines available by the bottle and 15 by the flute. The staff know their Asti Spumanti from their Bolly and tasting is allowed; if you're undecided try the Magic Flutes, a selection of three champagnes to help tickle your fancy.

All the mega-expensive Prestige Cuvee champagnes are served in Riedel Ouverture flutes. There's also a selection of appetisers, caviar and choccies from La Maison du Chocolat.

Oil paintings hang on the walls and the copper-topped bar is lined with stools, with sofas set up around low tables and in curtained-off alcoves. The candles are burning and pot plants add a bit of frondy greenness while you sit, sip and chat.

Wednesday night is jazz night and Thursday-Saturday DJs spin everything from the 1960s to now.

Courting couples will head for the alcoves but beware: the toilets are also behind a curtain and after a skinful you might also get an eyeful.

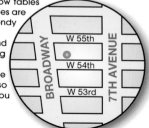

Foley's NY

Take me to: 18 W. 33rd St (between 5th Ave & Broadway)

THE ladies' room was only added in recent years because, in a previous life, this place was a brothel that served the original Waldorf=Astoria across the street. But the hotel was knocked down in 1929 so they could erect the Empire State Building.

Foley's is to baseball fans what sweetshops are to kids. Named after Red Foley, the former announcer at Yankees and Mets games who still pops in, it's "Where Everything is 6ft 2 and Even"; a phrase coined by former Red Sox coach Joe Morgan to describe someone with a hangover.

The walls are plastered top to bottom with signed baseball memorabilia, all of it donated to Yankee-fan owner Shaun Clancy.

Hanging from the ceiling are shirts from all sports, with plenty of British football clubs represented. There's even selected footy games on TV, with no cover charge. On tap you can choose from Sam Adams, Stella, Newcy Brown, Bud and Bud Light.

Foley's is busy at lunch and there's always scouts (of the baseball talent variety) and mlb.com staffers popping in.

Friday nights during the baseball season are a must as the place gets packed for the live games on TV.

Foley's crowning glory is the beautiful Tiffany stained glass in the restaurant which, along with the giant marble urinals, was rescued from the Waldorf=Astoria.

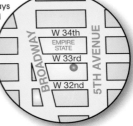

Jimmy's Corner

Take me to: 140 W. 44th St
(between Broadway & 6th Ave)

IN THE trade this place is quaintly known as a dive bar - but one thing owner Jimmy Glenn never took was a dive.

Jimmy is a former boxer who was beaten by Floyd Paterson as an amateur and was then in Paterson's corner when Muhammad Ali beat him in 1972.

His bar is the equivalent of a jab; short and in your face. It gets a bit cramped as you can stand two-deep at the bar at best.

The place is split in two with the bottom end laid out for diners. Jimmy's doesn't serve food but there's a shed-load of menus behind the bar from take-aways spots who will be happy to deliver.

All the beer's cold and cheap but you've more chance of going the distance with Jimmy than getting a freebie as they ain't big on the Buy Back. But it's a block away from Times Square and features an award-winning jukebox packed with Stax and jazz classics. In 2003 The Village Voice voted Jimmy's juke "The Best Jukebox to Impress Your Dad With".

Jimmy is usually around and maybe it's the size of his hands, but he's one of those people you instantly respect.

Join in the fun and sign a dollar bill which the barmaids will add to the collection. The majority are dedicated to Jimmy and sentiments range from "To Jimmy, Thank You, Bruce and Cheryl", to "John King (UK) eats too many pies".

The Rainbow Grill

Take me to: 30 Rockefeller Plaza, 65th floor (between W. 49th & W. 50th Sts)

THERE'S a very good reason why they charge the low teens for a bottle of Corona: it's right outside the windows. The Rainbow Grill has the best view of any bar in New York. Full stop. The end.

Everything south of W. 49th St is there in all its sky-scraping glory and the Rockefeller is the only place to get a decent view of the Empire State. And once the sun's gone down and the lights have come on, there's not a city in the world that can compete.

The Rainbow Grill offers a variety of nibbles and plenty of room for dining. At the bar there's space for about 12 but it's better to wait for a ring-side seat at the windows.

There's an extensive drinks menu and the bartenders can pour you anything you like, from their special house cocktails to a bottle of beer. Some bubbly, and house and premium wines are served by the glass, with the pricier plonk in bottles. Some of the prices are as gob-smacking as the view and it can work out cheaper to buy a bottle of some wines than two glasses.

But if you're felling as flush as John D. Rockefeller Jr himself, champers starts at just under $100 a bottle.

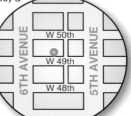

The place is reached by lift with entrances on 49th and 50th Sts. Inside the lobby you'll be met by door staff who'll only let you up if you're properly dressed. A jacket's required - leather will do - and jeans and trainers aren't allowed.

Grand Central Station & Chrysler Building, E. 42nd St

Bull and Bear Bar

Take me to: Waldorf=Astoria, 540 Lexington Ave (at 49th St)

THIS is where Masters of the Universe come to chew power lunches and drink expensive concoctions in between He-Man-sized bouts of money making. But despite the chaos you see on the trading floor, the fastest moving thing in here is the stock market ticker.

Named after the different types of market, the Bull and Bear has been attracting movers and shakers since it was The Men's Room pre-1960. Women weren't allowed before then but at the start of the swinging decade it was renamed.

It's as plush in an old-money-plush kinda way as you'd expect. The revolving door from Lexington spins you into a world of deep carpets and brass rails, paintings of thoroughbreds and weekends in The Hamptons. Tables and chairs are dotted around the dark wooden walls and a glass wall looks in on the restaurant where its legendary steaks are served.

The statues of a bull and bear stand nobly in the middle of the polished mahogany bar, its four sides curving inwards.

Beers come in stemmed glasses that aren't a pint but the bartenders will keep "refreshing" your drink at no extra charge. On tap you'll find Stella, Bud, Heineken and Sam Adams. But this is the stomping ground of wannabe Trumps, so splash the cash on something exotic. And tips in here are 15-20 per cent.

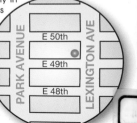

The Campbell Apartment

Take me to: Grand Central Station (Vanderbilt Ave entrance at 43rd St)

IF THE last time you missed the late train home you had to bunk up with Steve from sales on the benches at Crewe then this will be a pleasant surprise. Not only is this the most magnificent place you're likely to sip a Sidecar but it also has the comfiest bar stools in the world.

Located at the corner of Vanderbilt Ave and 43rd St, it was the private office of the super-wealthy John W. Campbell in the 1920s and '30s. And it's just as he left it and specialises in "Cocktails from another era".

It's wood panelled, 30ft wide by 60ft long, has a 25ft-high ceiling and a huge lead-glass window. Along with the super-comfy stools there are armchairs and banquettes for weary travellers to rest their bones.

Campbell decorated the room in the style of a 13th Century Florentine palace and filled it with furniture from that time and fine rugs. Nowadays it's kitted out with furniture from when Campbell was in residence. His safe still fills the large fireplace and the beautiful cabinets that once housed Tiffany diamonds and Faberge eggs now hold the Apartment's supply of booze.

After office hours the place is jumping as punters take their pick from champers, single malts and house speciality cocktails like Flapper's Delight and Robber Baron; while the Bloody Mary's have so much vodka in them they should be renamed Paper Cuts.

And you won't get in wearing jeans, trainers, sweatshirts, hoodies or shorts.

The Ginger Man

Take me to: 11 E. 36th St (between 5th & Madison Aves)

YOU can read the book, buy the t-shirt and probably even see the film as The Ginger Man is named after the comedy novel by J.P. Donleavy.

This beer-drinkers paradise sits in the shadow of the Empire State Building and at last count there were 63 draught and 160 bottles to choose from. As you'd expect the bartenders won't hassle you for a quick decision on your weapon of choice.

Take your pick from the best booze the world has to offer, including Orkney Skullsplitter, Young's Dirty Dick and Dogfish Head World Wide Stout in bottles; and Stone Brewing Arrogant Bastard, Spaten Optimator and Bud Light on tap.

Add to this a varied choice of single malt scotches, American and Irish whiskeys, champers and non-alcoholic beverages, and you'll see there's something to suit all tastes.

The Ginger Man is cavernous to look at but surprisingly cosy. Maybe it's the dark wood panelling, leather sofas and warm lighting; you decide.

There's a dartboard, waitress service, booths for dining and window seats for nursing a bottle of Mad Bitch while gazing up at the world's most famous skyscraper just two blocks away.

Popular after work, it has been known to get a bit loud so if your style's being cramped head to the lounge where the lighting is subdued, to say the least.

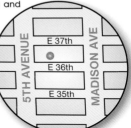

King Cole Bar & Lounge

Take me to: St Regis Hotel, 2 E. 55th St (between 5th and Madison Aves)

ACCORDING to legend the Bloody Mary was created here by Fernand Petiot in 1934. But the name was far too brutal for the St Regis' clientele and so it's still known here by this original moniker of the Red Snapper.

Petiot first mixed his creation in Harry's New York Bar in Paris back in the 1920s but refined his formula once he was Stateside; a move that has got him a mention on the Lea & Perrins website.

With such a famous mixological history the King Cole's barkeeps have to be at the top of their game; and these boys know more about rocket fuel than the eggheads who put Neil Armstrong on the Moon.

A 20ft-long mural by Maxfield Parrish of the Old King Cole nursery rhyme looks down from behind the bar on the merry old souls fiddling with their bling in-between slugs of a Big Apple Martini.

There are no draught beers and yes, they really can get away with charging that much for a bottle of Budweiser. And you'll be pleased to hear in places this posh you tip at least 15%.

King Cole is accessed via the restaurant, down the steps, past the piano and through the glass doors. And a jacket-required policy is enforced.

You know it's posh when the snacks contain wasabi peas. But don't fret over that urban myth about pee on the bar snacks in a place: the people here wash their hands, or can afford to pay a man to do it for them.

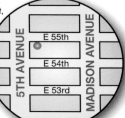

Pen-Top Bar & Terrace

Take me to: Peninsula Hotel, 700 5th Ave (at 55th St)

THE bar isn't the only thing that's high as the prices are a bit steep, too. But you are sitting on the roof of an elegant hotel and as any half-decent estate agent will tell you, you're paying for the view.

Take the express lift to this eyrie 23 floors up for views of Fifth Avenue in all its fabulousnesss, with Central Park visible just four blocks north.

Basically, the Pen-Top is a posh conservatory with tinted glass and views on three sides. At the bar are high leather chairs and dotted around are tables for two. But the wrought-iron furniture on the terrace is where you want to be, weather permitting.

The actual bar has been likened to an ice cube and the counter top is made from half-inch-thick glass tiles a foot square that are lit from underneath. You'd spoil it by installing beer pumps so there's no draught and the uber-expensive bottled stock runs to Stella, Heineken, Amstel Light and Coors Light.

They have their own range of Fifth Avenue Cocktails like the Big Apple Martini, which comes with a dash of Sprite. Champagne and house wines are served by the glass or bottle and there's a selection of imported cheeses for your delectation.

This elegant vantage point is the sort of spot from which Batman has launched many a crime-fighting caper, which is spookily handy as the place opened in 1905 as The Gotham Hotel.

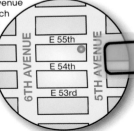

P.J. Clarke's

Take me to: 915 3rd Ave (at 55th St)

ANOTHER classic New York saloon run by friendly Irish folk. Opened in 1884, the two-storey building occupies its own corner plot and looks like the sort of place Don Corleone's boys used to screech up outside before spilling Mafioso claret with a quick burst from their Thompsons.

Nowadays you won't end up sleeping with the fishes but you can tuck into a selection of fresh seafood from the raw bar, or order one of their outstanding burgers if you prefer your meat red.

The interior is all original, from the mottled mirrors with dark wood surrounds, to the bar itself, the brass foot rail and tiled floor. And P.J. Clarke's wins the award for the coolest-looking Gents in the world, washed-hands down. It looks like an Edwardian tram shelter, complete with a stained-glass roof and houses two giant marble urinals.

There's the obligatory wide selection of spirits and Guinness, Boddies, Grolsch, Leffe Blonde and Stella by the pint. Magners, Budweiser and Beck's come in bottles.

In days gone by super celebs like Sinatra propped up the bar and the place has always played host to the after-work crowd in this tourist-free area of the city.

Food is available until 3am, with the dessert menu offering the delights of rice pudding, apple cobbler, pumpkin pie, and choc-chip cookie souffle. The backroom holds a restaurant, as does the upstairs which is accessed on 55th St.

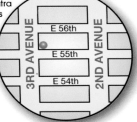

Strawberry Fields, Central Park

STRAWBERRY
FIELDS

Bemelmans Bar

Take me to: The Carlyle Hotel, 35 E. 76th St (at Madison Ave)

IF YOU drew on the walls you'd probably get arrested; Madeline creator Ludwig Bemelmans got a year's free room and board for his handiwork. Painted in 1947, the murals cover all the walls and depict the seasons in Central Park, along with Madeline and her classmates.

Bemelmans Bar is one of the most inviting places to get a drink ever and coupled with the cosy lighting, the artwork makes it seem like a nursery for grown-ups. All that's missing is a height chart.

All the seating is leather, from the curved banquettes along the walls to the chairs at the bar and the glass-topped, brass-rimmed tables.

Opened in 1930, The Carlyle is a stunning example of Art Deco and the perfect setting for a romantic cocktail. Martinis and wines are as popular as ever and the cocktail menu was created by Dale DeGroff and Audrey Saunders, two legends of their craft.

The walls are Bemelmans' only commission open to the public and were spruced up in 2001 when the repro lamp shades were added. The whole place is a jazz hot spot and Eartha Kitt is a regular performer, while Woody Allen was in residence for a large part of 2006.

The Carlyle is one block from Central Park. To get to Bemelmans veer left from the beautiful lobby past the lifts and then take a right; go up the steps through the small restaurant and then up the steps at the doorway.

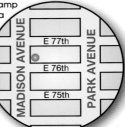

Central Park Boathouse

Take me to: Central Park
(at E. 72nd St & Park Drive North)

THERE'S nothing quite like messing about in boats. If you've worked up a thirst walking around Central Park then this is the perfect picturesque pick-me-up to sit and sip your favourite tipple - and watch other people get messed about in their vessel.

On your Central Park map it'll be listed as the Loeb Boathouse on the eastern tip of The Lake but just follow the Korean wedding party as I guarantee they'll be taking a rowboat out for a spin. And this post-nuptials "It's a Knockout" is all visible from a bar stool.

The Boathouse was built around 1874 but burned down and was replaced in the 1950s. This building is a classy mix of dark wood, white walls and stone floors, complete with a log fire to warm your cockles.

There are high chairs at the bar and the tables dotted about, leather wing-back chairs by the fire and comfy leather armchairs lined up below the bar looking out over the restaurant, which looks out over the water.

During the warmer months the large windows lining the front of The Boathouse are opened to let the breeze in, and the noise of the bonhomie from the outdoor bar & grill, which is open from summer until after November's marathon.

To find The Boathouse head in from Fifth Ave & 72nd St. You can also hop on The Boathouse Trolley, which picks up on Fifth at 72nd and 80th every 15 minutes.

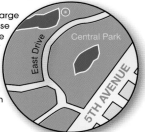

The Roof Garden

Take me to: Met. Museum of Art, 1000 5th Ave (at 82nd St)

IF YOU fancy spending an unhurried hour or two gazing at Central Park in all its autumnal glory, while sipping a livener before having your picture taken by the Assyrian Reliefs on the second floor, you're in luck.

One of New York's best-kept secrets quietly goes about its business on top of one of its most popular landmarks. This baby gives you an unbroken 180-degree panorama of "New York's heart", although it's ticker may be a bit dicky as there's a smoking area up here.

The terrace is used for modern art exhibitions and bordered by a neatly-clipped hedge. The bar itself is little more than a well-stocked trolley with bottled beers, wine and spirits, and also sells butties, soup and Haagen-Dazs.

There's plenty of seating around the edges and in the shade by the bar. The Roof Garden is open from May-October and is accessible only by one lift - so pay attention.

From the main entrance on Fifth walk straight ahead to Medieval Art. Once there take a left and go through European Sculpture and Decorative Arts. The lift is just by the entrance to Arts of Africa, Oceania and the Americas.

Once inside feel free to wander about and admire the priceless collections. Admission isn't free but it won't hurt to pay the less-than-$20 "recommended" fee.

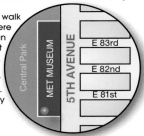

Tavern on the Green

Take me to: Central Park (at W. 67th St)

BEFORE bling there was the Tavern on the Green. Imagine six of the layers of Hell decorated by Liberace. But a trip to New York wouldn't be complete without a visit to the garden bar at this former sheep barn. And "Ghostbusters" was filmed here.

Built in 1870, the Victorian Gothic building was used to house the 200 sheep that grazed on the nearby Sheep Meadow. In 1934 it was converted into a restaurant and opened in its present incarnation on August 31, 1976. The brains behind that two-year, $10million revamp was Warner LeRoy, the ebullient grandson of Warner Bros. founder Harry.

There are six OTT restaurants under one roof here. The Crystal Pavilion, Chestnut Room, Park Room, the Rafters Room, the Terrace Room and the Crystal Room, which looks out over NYC's largest outdoor bar.

Open from June-September the bar is stocked with 28 vodkas, 12 tequilas, 21 single malts and beers including Stella, Bud and Beck's. Hanging baskets jostle with Chinese lanterns, which come on at night as the garden turns into a disco.

There is a bar inside but it's no more than a room where diners are kept in an holding pattern until their table is ready.

As the Tavern is on City Park Property there's no dress code, despite ongoing complaints about the scruff at the next table in flip-flops. But as it's so dazzling inside, it might be nice to make an effort.

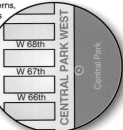

Index

Tribeca & South

THE BUBBLE LOUNGE
228 W. Broadway (between
Franklin and N. Moore St)
Mon-Thu 5pm-2am;
Fri, Sat 5pm-4am.
bubblelounge.com

BRANDY LIBRARY
25 N. Moore St (between
W. Broadway & Hudson St)
4pm-4am.
brandylibrary.com

ULYSSES'
95 Pearl St/58 Stone St
(at Hanover Sq)
11am-4am.
ulyssesbarnyc.com

SoHo

BROOME ST BAR
363 W. Broadway
(corner of Broome St)
11am-2am.

CIRCA TABAC
32 Watts St (between
W. Broadway & 6th Ave)
5pm-4am.

EAR INN
326 Spring St (between
Greenwich & Washington Sts)
11.30am-4am.
jamesbrownhouse.com

PUCK FAIR
298 Lafayette St (between
Houston & Prince Sts)
11.30am-4am.
ulyssesbarnyc.com

West Village & Meatpacking

CHUMLEY'S
86 Bedford St (between
Barrow & Grove Sts)
Mon-Thu 4pm-midnight;
Fri, Sat noon-1.30am;
Sun 3pm-midnight.

THE CUBBYHOLE
281 W. 12th St (at 4th St)
Mon-Fri 4pm-4am;
Sat, Sun 2pm-4am.
members.aol.com/cubbyhole1

DUBLIN 6
575 Hudson St (between
W. 11th and Bank Sts)
Mon-Fri 5pm-midnight;
Sat, Sun noon-4am.
dublin6nyc.com

EMPLOYEES ONLY
510 Hudson St (at Christopher St)
6pm-4am.
employeesonlynyc.com

GASLIGHT
400 W. 14th St
(at 9th Ave)
1pm-4am.
gaslightnyc.com

HENRIETTA HUDSON BAR & GIRL
438 Hudson St (at Morton St)
Mon-Fri 3pm-4am;
Sat, Sun 1pm-4am.
henriettahudson.com

HUDSON BAR & BOOKS
636 Hudson St (at Horatio St)
Mon-Wed 5pm-3am;
Thu-Sat 5pm-4am; Sun 5pm-3am.
barandbooks.cz

PLUNGE
Hotel Gansevoort, 18 9th Ave
(at 13th St)
11am-4am.
hotelgansevoort.com

THE STONEWALL
53 Christopher St (between
Waverley Pl & 7th Ave South)
3pm-4am
stonewall-place.com

WHITE HORSE TAVERN
567 Hudson St (at 11th St)
Mon-Thu 11am-1.30am; Fri, Sat
11am-3.30am; Sun 11am-1.30am.

Greenwich Village

MADAME X
94 W. Houston St (between
La Guardia Pl & Thompson St)
Mon-Fri 6pm-4am;
Sat, Sun 7pm-4am.
madamexnyc.com

MARION'S CONTINENTAL
RESTAURANT & LOUNGE
354 Bowery (between
Great Jones & E. 4th Sts)
Mon-Thu 5.30pm-2am; Fri, Sat
5.30pm-3am; Sun 5pm-midnight.
marionsnyc.com

PECULIER PUB
145 Bleecker St (between
Thompson St & La Guardia Pl)
Mon-Thu 5pm-1am;

Fri 3.30pm-4am; Sat 2pm-4am;
Sun 4pm-4am.

SWIFT HIBERNIAN LOUNGE
34 E. 4th St (between
Bowery & Lafayette St)
Noon-4am.
ulyssesbarnyc.com

TEMPLE BAR
332 Lafayette (between
Bleecker & Houston Sts)
Mon-Thu 5pm-1am; Fri, Sat
5pm-2am.
templebarnyc.com

East Village

ACE BAR
531 E. 5th St (between
Aves A & B)
4pm-4am.
acebar.com

ANGEL'S SHARE
8 Stuyvesant St (between
3rd Ave & 9th St)
6pm-2.30am.

BURP CASTLE
41 E. 7th St (between
2nd & Bowery)

Mon-Thu 5pm-2am; Fri 5pm-4am;
Sat 4pm-4am; Sun 6pm-2am.

KGB BAR
85 E. 4th St (between
Bowery & 2nd Ave)
7pm-4am.
kgbbar.com

McSORLEY'S
15 E. 7th St (between
2nd & 3rd Aves)
Mon-Sat 11am-1am; Sun
1pm-1am.
mcsorleysnewyork.com

NEVADA SMITH'S
74 3rd Ave (between
11th & 12th Sts)
Mon-Fri noon-4am;
*Sat 7.30am-4am;
*Sun 8am-4am.
(*during football season).
grahamecurtis.com/
nevadasmiths/index.html

THE SUNBURNT COW
137 Ave C (between 8th & 9th Sts)
Mon-Thu 6pm-2am; Fri 6pm-4am;
Sat noon-4am; Sun
noon – midnight.
thesunburntcow.com

TELEPHONE BAR & GRILL
149 2nd Ave (between
9th & 10th Sts)
Mon-Thu 11.30am-2am; Fri, Sat
11.30am-3am; Sun 10am-1am.
telebar.com

VELVET CIGAR LOUNGE
80 E. 7th St (between
1st & 2nd Aves)
Mon-Fri 4pm-2am; Sat noon-2am;
Sun noon-midnight.
velvetcigars.com

ZUM SCHNEIDER
107 Ave C (at 7th St)
Mon-Fri 5pm-4am; Sat, Sun
1pm-4am.
zumschneider.com

Chelsea

BARRACUDA
275 W. 22nd St (between
7th & 8th Aves)
4pm-4am.

BRITE BAR
297 10th Ave (at 27th St)
Tues-Fri 5.30pm-4am; Sat 7pm-
4am; Sun 8pm-4am.
britebar.com

FLATIRON LOUNGE
37 W. 19th St (between
5th & 6th Aves)
Sun-Wed 5pm-2am;
Thu-Sat 5pm-4am.
flatironlounge.com

G LOUNGE
225 W. 19th St (between
7th & 8th Aves)
4pm-4am.
glounge.com

GYM SPORTS BAR
167 8th Ave (between
18th & 19th Sts)
Mon-Thu 4pm-2am;
Fri 4pm-4am;
Sat 1pm-4am; Sun 1pm-2am.
gymsportsbar.com

THE HALF KING
505 W. 23rd St (between
10th & 11th Aves)
9am-4am.
thehalfking.com

SERENA
Chelsea Hotel, 222 W. 23rd St
(between 7th & 8th Aves)
Tue-Fri 6pm-4am; Sat 7pm-4am.
serenanyc.com

TRAILER PARK LOUNGE & GRILL
271 W. 23rd St (between
7th & 8th Aves)
Noon-3am.
trailerparklounge.com

Gramercy & Flatiron

BEAUTY BAR
231 E. 14th St (between
2nd & 3rd Aves)
Sun-Thu 5pm-4am; Fri, Sat
7pm-4am.
beautybar.com

OLD TOWN BAR & GRILL
45 E. 18th St (between
Broadway & Park Ave South)
Mon-Sat noon-1am; Sun 3pm-1am.
oldtownbar.com

PETE'S TAVERN
129 E. 18th St (at Irving Place)
11.15am-3am.
petestavern.com

Midtown West

BRYANT PARK CAFE & GRILL

25 W. 40th St (between
5th & 6th Aves)
11.30am-11pm.
bryantpark.org

CELLAR BAR
The Bryant Park, 40 W. 40th St
(between 5th & 6th Aves)
Mon 5pm-midnight; Tue, Wed
5pm-1pm; Thu 5pm-3am; Fri
5pm-4am; Sat 8pm-4am.
bryantparkhotel.com

ESPN ZONE
1472 Broadway (at 42nd St)
Mon, Tue, Thu 11.30am-12.30am;
Wed 11am-12.30am; Fri, Sat
11am-1am; Sun 11am-midnight.
espnzone.com/newyork

FLUTE
205 W. 54th St (between
Broadway & 7th Ave)
Sun-Wed 5pm-2am; Thu
5pm-3am; Fri, Sat 5pm-4am.
flutebar.com

FOLEY'S NY
18 W. 33rd St (between
5th & Broadway)
Mon-Sat 11am-2am; Sun
noon-2am.

JIMMY'S CORNER
140 W. 44th St (between
Broadway & 6th Ave)
Mon-Sat 11am-4am; Sun
noon-4am.

RAINBOW GRILL
30 Rockefeller Plaza, 65th Floor
(between W. 49th & W. 50th Sts)
Sun-Thu 5pm-midnight; Fri, Sat
5pm-1am.
rainbowroom.com/rainbow_grill

Midtown East

**BULL and BEAR BAR
& STEAKHOUSE**
Waldorf=Astoria,
540 Lexington Ave (at 49th St)
Spring/Summer Mon-Fri
noon-11.30pm; Sat,
Sun 5pm-11.30pm; Autumn/Winter
noon-11.30pm.
hilton.com

THE CAMPBELL APARTMENT
Grand Central Station,
15 Vanderbilt Ave Entrance
Mon-Sat 3pm-1am; Sun
3pm-11pm.
grandcentralterminal.com

THE GINGER MAN

11 E. 36th St (between
5th & Madison Aves)
Mon-Wed 11.30am-2am; Thu, Fri
11.30am-4am; Sat 12.30pm-4am;
Sun 3pm-midnight.
gingerman-ny.com

KING COLE BAR & LOUNGE

St Regis Hotel, 2 E. 55th St
(between 5th & Madison Aves)
Mon-Thu 11.30am-1am; Fri, Sat
11.30am-2am; Sun noon-midnight.
starwoodhotels.com/stregis

PEN-TOP BAR & TERRACE

Peninsula Hotel, 700 5th Ave
(at 55th St)
Mon-Thu 5pm-midnight;
Fri, Sat 5pm-1am.
newyork.peninsula.com

P. J. CLARKE'S

915 3rd Ave (at 55th St)
11am-4am.
pjclarkes.com

The Uppers

BEMELMANS BAR

The Carlyle Hotel, 35 E. 76th St
(at Madison Ave)
11am-1am.
thecarlyle.com

THE BOATHOUSE

Central Park, E 72nd St &
Park Drive North
Mon-Fri 10.30am-11pm;
Sat, Sun 10.30am-midnight.
Outside bar: 11am-11pm
(Apr-Nov, weather permitting).
thecentralparkboathouse.com

THE ROOF GARDEN

Metropolitan Museum of Art,
1000 5th Ave (at 82nd St)
Sun 10am-4.30pm;
Tue-Thu 10am-4.30pm;
Fri, Sat 10am-8.30pm.
metmuseum.org

TAVERN ON THE GREEN

Central Park (at W. 67th St
11.30am-midnight.
tavernonthegreen.com

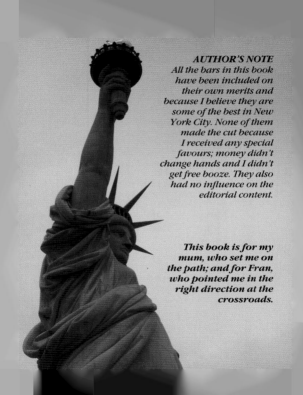

AUTHOR'S NOTE
*All the bars in this book
have been included on
their own merits and
because I believe they are
some of the best in New
York City. None of them
made the cut because
I received any special
favours; money didn't
change hands and I didn't
get free booze. They also
had no influence on the
editorial content.*

*This book is for my
mum, who set me on
the path; and for Fran,
who pointed me in the
right direction at the
crossroads.*